# Oracular Maladies

# ORACULAR MALADIES

Poems by SOPHIA TERAZAWA

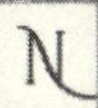

ISBN 978-1-955992-70-1

PUBLISHED BY NOEMI PRESS, INC.
A NONPROFIT LITERARY ORGANIZATION
WWW.NOEMIPRESS.ORG

COVER AND INTERIOR DESIGN
BY ALBAN FISCHER

"They tortured you, and you confessed only to a love beyond measure for the causes of your torture."

—Mahmoud Darwish, *tr. Ibrahim Muhawi*

"Soldier, the dawn is icy."

—Dương Thu Hương, *tr. Phan Huy Đường & Nina McPherson*

# CONTENTS

## SCORE IV



## SCORE V

*Though the original text for* ORACULAR MALADIES *was composed in cicada-speak, with particular focus on Japanese mōra-timed metrical verse, our interpreters have taken liberties with some of the more delicate expressions. None of this new work corresponds with the old, therefore, an entirely separate production; the following curses have little to no commercial value.*

ミンミン

# SYNOPSIS

These are scores and character studies of episodes from a beloved musical variety show beginning in 1983. Paris.

Live production travels west, for the most part, in a zigzag pattern akin to a heat-seeking missile, moving first to Cerritos, California, and then off to Las Vegas, Los Angeles, Houston, Toronto, Long Beach, a triumphant return to Paris, juddering back across the water to Buena Park, San Jose, Atlanta, Houston, Seoul, and on and so forth . . .

American desert casino resorts give way to boutique hotels, exclusive plastic surgery consultations, shuttle buses, and pop. Philharmonic concert halls glimmer with tuxedos, embroidered silk sleeves, and sequins. Sequins are everywhere. Carefully timed confetti burst from the rafters. Producers, beet-orange in the face, are shouting names into megaphones between sets. Binders of casting sheets snap open and shut. Props stick together on the tongue. I can only recognize a simple phrase here and there. "Please hurry."

"Go, now."

Studio lights flash over many trap doors. Cameras on dollies glide past each other. The drama unfolds in variations of the same story: a coffee-stained letter penned on the raised knee of a seated soldier onstage.

*In a few select episodes, there will be opportunities for audience participation. Signs will illuminate off-stage indicating when to* LAUGH, CLAP, *or* SIGH.

"Em," says the dark outline, age 22, breaking into song.

The performance sharpens with a spotlight. The face comes into focus. Sepia behind black hair billows to violins and a soft artificial breeze, an audible gasp from the audience as our soldier is revealed to be played by the ruinously handsome DIVO, Danny Nguyễn.

"Today," warbles the DIVO.

With a word close to love, he's clutching a patriotic fist to his chest. He's gazing toward Camera Two which cross-fades onto the sheet of paper draped over his knee and, after some seconds, toward a far, far unknown in 1968. Saigon.

"Today," sings our DIVO one last time.

"I hold your portrait in my mind and remember peaceful hours passing by. Please tell your mother how sorry I feel, though my heart is clear and my body, strong."

*Flash title card:*

xa xa xa lắm

*Cast in order of appearance:*

K. Ly . . . . . . . . . . DIVA
T. Lam . . . . . . . . . . DIVA
N. Quỳnh . . . . . . . . . . DIVA
Đ. Nguyên . . . . . . . . . . DIVO
D. Hồ . . . . . . . . . . DIVO
Q. Lê . . . . . . . . . . DIVO
Kenzo . . . . . . . . . . KENZO
Chị Ba (pseud.) . . . . . . . . . . AUNT
Anh Hai (pseud.) . . . . . . . . . . UNCLE
Chị Tám (pseud.) . . . . . . . . . . MOTHER
— . . . . . . . . . . DAUGHTER
Bò . . . . . . . . . . BÒ
C. Nguyễn . . . . . . . . . . HOST
N. Nguyễn . . . . . . . . . . HOST

# SCORE I

# EN EMINENCE

*an intarsia*

Wait offstage. A potted taro's exposed
shoots [Psyche, as told by Apuleius]

[à]

*What a day*—you paraphrase her second task

[à]

Down in the reeds, multiple characters forget their
lines. Silhouetted divas cut to fleece

[à]

[Golden] crickets signal withal but

[à]

Cue autumnal rebellions caught on tape.
As gathering fiber, our colony sings. Who

[à]

In this, collects enough to meet retelling

[à]

Divas signal "gold" in short, difficult
movements. Choose among four sacred

[à]

Animals and occupation at sea, the dolphin

[à]

Sealing up her eyes. You play our tape.
Tumble reaching, elders poison [offer]

[à]

In our colony, impossible lyrics to memorize

[ȁ]

Divas die out. Ask, not saying, “Mai,
the dawn!” Cue shimmering by final proof

[ȁ]

I, who forgot a line about water

[ȁ]

Swim harpooned to the chest. When you go
who can I sing for? Bergamot in groves

[ȁ]

As a pod, compelled to lose a sense

[ȁ]

Sonar, leading through this dark which none
know not of doubling, I greet whoever curses me.

# SPEAR BEARER

Had it been imperfect
tempered by oil staining

Kiyoko's scroll
horrid beige,
no calendar would have

as we do in this sentence.
Gather today. Feast.

One might hunt
in groups
bent to despair our world.

You might be that
enemy offshore, sailing in.

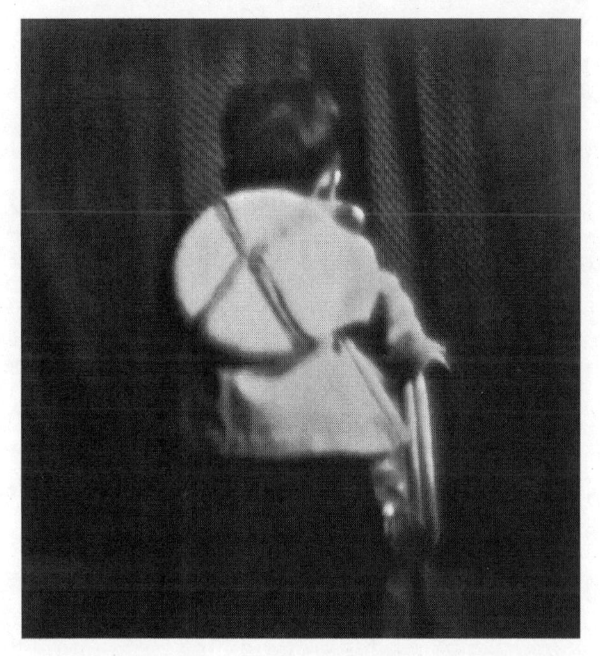

# ["MAI, THE DAWN!"]

*a short film*

Insects trill
darkened frames.

Fade in: DIVA sits
behind netting. Twilight.

Đàn nguyệt. Two-stringed
moon parlays her voice

accompanied by subtitles:
*Where did you fall? When you*

*fell, did a nightingale*
*appear?* Cut to montage.

Camphor, warbler on
twigs careening away,

et cetera. *True,* she says.
*They exacted us*

*to speak. Did you speak?*
Don't answer that. Go

concealed in lamps stained
annatto orange. Then

suppose this dawn
nine generations ago

was truly icy,
bone brittle, would you

walk north on your knees
toward the Forbidden Gates?

Would it take a month?
At the prison, would you

beat your chest calling
out your son's name?

Cut to montage. Agar-
wood chips fluttering,

hand opening a book,
et cetera. Suppose

our torturers left
long before this.

Do you understand?
A pre-recorded sound:

*Applause, far, far*
*away like locusts*

*cut from paper.* You
laugh but don't know why.

*ó ộ iề a a a ắ*

*ó ộ iề ê ôi ê ắ*

*iế á ơi iê ỡ ia à ôi*

# SUPPOSE A LUTE

We dance in our best heels through the old quarter
lined with blossoms: peach,
pear, mountain-ebony, plum, apricot.

Your brother's tuning a lute peg off-scale.
He stays beyond Tết with this
cobblestone music. Perhaps he'll twine

soot-covered thread around our ankles,
your dead husband, too.
Could it be possible, describing sugar without

terms close to *sweet?* This year becomes
good dyed pink, fortunate for all who ask.

# SCORE II

# HEART MURMUR

*a ballad*

Pairs of divas enter
stage right, stage left. Cut to
live audience squeezed together.
Rows in a grand casino fog.

Near the back, alone,
mouthing along: mother-elder,
light shepherding news from home.
*Not good*, she says. Enter cello

carried on incomplete measures.
*But when I look at you,* answers a diva,
*I cry*. Toning her song,
vast, mistaken for pearls.

# THE CELLIST

Tall as Kenzo at two

deciding if a bird
could be enough

à voix basse,

called to say
clouds take every shape

though one

with all this wind
and Kenzo,

who's not my child yet

padding across our stage,
turned quiet.

Kenzo, come here.

# [“XA XA XA LẮM”]

*live performance after a song of the same title*

At Chị Ba’s. Waco, Texas. On VHS
our hosts arrange pyramids of apricots. Cut to
someone across the street glancing through
a tinted fossil shop window. Who wears
a child’s Santa hat, taffy pink gloves
pulled past the elbows? Who distills that
motion, if observed long enough, an allegory?

Divas lip-sync onstage. Was in lieu of
leaving their fault, a refugee, or both? One
becomes my aunt. Enter AUNT in wide
angle shots. Flickers form infinite
possibilities cast on the screen. AUNT
enters a room. She sits awake all night.
*If you enter,* she says. *I’ll shoot.* UNCLE,

played by her first boyfriend in America,
fades in. He stands outside like a comma
at the door, looking in, squaring the audience.

# BÒ: BACKCHANNEL, VOLLEY OF SONGS

*mise-en-scène*

Track MOTHER and DAUGHTER, crab walking
to their seats. [Camera spins.] Three guards,
uniformed, eat bánh mì out of white paper bags.

Motion their country on tape.
Syllables volley back and forth.

~~~

The show starts late. Your uncle weeps in the auditorium.
He clutches an armrest, letting his tears, a warless badge,
fall from his face.

~~~

DIVA [onstage] and MOTHER magnetize.

ˋˋˋ

Chorus: I toggle between glossaries
shining a betel seed. Such is a myth of ours.

She whorls with the camera. Enter BÒ
played by a live cow. BÒ, just standing there.

Music, arrhythmic sung-
spoken at the same time: No, no fire.

Who's the guard who cries? Not me.

*o ườ ài ó ộ ì ôi*

*ê ầu ời ộ ầ ă ơ ôi*

*ôi ở ề ưới á ao ơi*

# ["WHO GHOST-LOCKS ME?"]

You scatter to sea, my grain, simply hearing of charity, encompassing the dreams, ambling or stated simply harvesting, or given, hopefully to shore. Scarlet history ties history trigger, ever-wincing camouflage half-        open, burnt through        canopy, to whistle for                your whistle

# ["THROUGH BURNT CANOPIES, A FOOTNOTE WHISTLES OVERHEAD"]

*after Nhã Thuyên*

Through burnt canopies, a footnote whistles overhead, perhaps the trees, grunting, the sapling near my thigh, kneecaps casting sweet magnolia to din, sweetened jade, perhaps a trickle, shadowing the earth, earthly like the chest, at night, separating you from palm from lip, pulls up warmth or tonguing it, pronounce it yet the possibilities for grief, coloring my body in as much, bodies coloring divide, my bodily collapse, backing jungles, where, collapsing after sap, quickens in my human, thick of jungle forcing braids, jungles braid desire to my reclamation, fire, forging

echoes in my mouth, lunging after bombs, sapling, thatched roof, amber, hardened eyes, glimmering eyes, forgiving eyes, collecting, infinitely harder, brighter than the amber, giving alms forgiving, kissing me, I ask the gravestones, why forgive our dead, holding a mangrove, wish for alms, whispering our resolve into my being, then you glisten, glistening, my voices multiply beneath duress, you wrap me, wrapping me in burning leaves, the way a country's flesh grows back, the seeping after warding off your color, lifting me, the monsoon, laying me among your ashen temples, gazing, quietly, your afternoon upon my face, I wash the rice for lunch, my face, the other coloring divide, the coloring of braids, desiring some reclamation, longing after bombs, long despite that echo, bombing, sapling, thatched roof, amber, hardened eyes, glimmering eyes, forgiving eyes, collecting, infinitely harder, brighter than the amber, giving alms forgiving, thick of jungle forcing braids to separate, right then you walk into my home then kiss me, why forgive the dead, my gravestones ask, gashing, entering, your interest holds resolve against my being noted yellow for its copper, browning stones, whirring, stirring afternoons to gazes tender, like you, tenderly believing, love, the grief for what it gives to justice, vivid cities, vivid music, fracturing my spirit, fracturing the music, recognizing under your illuminating gaps, the gapping to peace, inheritance by pieces, waning off my lighted gaps, illuminating gaps, admitting, learning not to love a grief for what it gives to justice, commonly avoided, practiced in the margins, safely in the margins, committed to its margins, braiding my desire to some reclamation, long, in spite of longing echoes, longing after bombs, sapling, thatched roof, amber, hardened eyes, glimmering eyes, forgiving eyes, collecting, infinitely harder, brighter than the

amber, giving alms forgiving, thick
right then you walk into my home
my gravestones ask, shimmering,
to the jute thus frozen, sunlight thus
hours shouldering embrace, freezing
light, colossal veils snaking up trees,
day, night, two hundred fingers
for what it gives, uprooted, day by
embrace, shouldering these bounds
waken up the dead, dusking, the
inked, cups upon your making or
grief, what it gives to ink, the
shoulders, crossing out this love,
the ink of knotted up, by tones, the

of jungles forcing me to separate,
then kiss me, why forgive the dead,
then brighter, frozen like the sapling
collides, your shoulders bending,
out the war or veiling with your
the snakes become those trees, over
break the ground, you love a grief
day, decanters hours shouldering
to optic nerve to run, to jolt, to
making of your light constitutionally
accounting for the love far beyond a
shouldering of weight upon your
knotted up your love, crossing out
melanin to brown, shutting up the

housing, hovering the spill of hours shouldering embrace, you pause, breathing, safer, *home as sound returns to sunrise,* holding, ambling my days to state lines given all the rays, cleansing jungles, tapping jungles, felling out the jungle, that forgiving jungle, buried in my jungles, lost inside your jungle, tangled with my jungles, tangled with the loving grief for what it gives, for what it shores up with divide upon arrival, older feats of weary, hopelessly, you're pulling out the navigational account of poetry, the fragments loving grief for what it gives to justice, practiced in the margins, safely, there, committed to your margins, may you be, instead, contracted, yes, asylum is a place we never cross into each other, gapped, loving the grief for what it gives to justice negates my widening divide, loving a grief for what it gives to justice, receding from faces possibilities of color, memories that ache with confidential tones, hence you destroy, deforest after color, tearing up to shades, loving grief for what it gives to color, here, atop another color spackling my tears, you love the grief for what it gives to trapezoids or squares, for are you in my skyline, in my freedom, are you in your freedom or my freedom, spirited to music, cities fractured, spirited to fractures, cities, music, there, you pull out first the navigational account of poetry, the leaving count, you turn my heart in rhythms bursting into walls, slowing the light down, here, dissolving, loving grief for what it gives to justice, bursting where you stop, you stop the jungle after rain, loving the grief for what it gives to justice, winding, nowhere leaves the hour, hourly of broken, cups, collecting all the flood, immense as flooding cities gutted into floods, matrimony, you are ambling divide, dividing up my path, maybe, wherefore, the fated makes it stop, naming your time unstoppable, you slash at all the overgrowth, that loves a grief for what it gives, desires reclamation, long after the echo, longing after bombs, sapling, thatched roof, amber, hardened eyes, glimmering eyes, forgiving eyes, collecting, infinitely harder, brighter than the amber, giving alms forgiving, thicker with the jungle, thick, like loving grief for what it gives, to force a braid to separate, right then you walk into my home then kiss me, why forgive the dead, my gravestones ask, shimmering much brighter, frozen, sapling with their jute, frozen like the sunlight, here, colliding with your shoulders bending under hour, all embracing, shouldering my stones with your wall, where you break it, shouldering the stones but stones are never really stones, moving roundly, ghostly, you are diplomatically most plural, leaving, millions to hunger boats, shattering to sea, home as sound returning to sunrise, fading like witness stops surrendering to jungle, exiting inheritance for what you know exists, twisting most carefully, destroys, takes over, has no way of stopping, moves as though to stop my home as silence after sunrise, there, you love me, grief for what it gives, the hummingbirds must fall from skies, you listen now to multiply, you listen up to multiply, holding up to multiply, you multiply, the laying down to multiply, the lifting me to multiply, the whispering divide, kissing, multiplying shoulders in the knots of forests gazing through my cups, out here, believing me, racing up our trees, chests at night dividing palm from lip, what pulls out warmly, shouldering embrace, bending fractures, might illuminate the gapping, counting up your layers, navigationally poetry, you love a grief for what it gives to banishment, speaking the wind, most gloriously emerald, hesitating, marginal, birthing the month, at last, diluted colors, touching near the margins, birthing up a month, diluted by its colors, humming, leaving, eyes jolt to the run, *home as sound returns to sunrise,* you must marry, move out of the stones, loving grief for what it gives to justice, my beloved, is this meeting required?

# ["HOW MIGHT YOU BE ATTENTIVE TO MY LIVING?"]

blue transforms
mourning

cesspool into
light

holes     feverishly
render

một tờ giấy
sheets of earth

thrum-thrum
diamond     tongue

một ly nước
spells tipping over

*[deep vibrato]*

## ["MESH IS PINK, TAFFETA BEDAZZLED"]

Mesh is pink, taffeta bedazzled with their ruby on-stage. Plastic shoes are colored; neon covers stage. Sequined DIVAS walk through thunder. Massively, their chrome steel is laced with beads, molten near the light. Platforms sink on tape, into each covered holes, leaving quiet signs for an audience to ponder then abide by quietly, applause. Therefore, DIVAS rise all their arms waving like trees.

*[fog machine]*

## ["CAN YOU DESCRIBE THE SOUND?"]

sấm sét      dreams
gathering up

domes

đi hát           mưa
clinging to a pause

Thanh Lam

plucks      every string
gourd hollows out

*[sound of clapping]*

# RESIDUAL

These syllables strike our lower
register [branching: fog]. Who whispers
like a friend, "Bêche-de-mer,"

I wring out towels and pillow cases.
Sunday afternoon. Check on
your sister, you sign. She won't speak

anymore. Glass trees.
Soapstone box. You package her father's
old shirt there in Queens

[arms crossed at the chest] posing
unpalatably. I imitate you
imitating him like a tourist on the tenth

night of spring in a country bent
to numb what could hurt but doesn't.

# ORACLES, UNTENDED

If you must know our language,
there's a field some call a garden.

Go there if you can.

Back to subjects of want,
never have we seen so many flowers.

Here's a plate and gardens beyond.

*Paleo-*

You walk to our city of torture, reign
from simple joy. A vesper drum

most serenely carries, if it should,

inflection.

May you not tire so soon.

*Meso-*

I forget to say

he, such desire drapes

Đại
on a horse.

*Neo-*

May our divas sing
untended

by night. You glance upon the cabinet.

*Paleo-*

Seals collected, ransacked, a treasure,
no subject is joy spread about its sentence. You walk

two concubines behind.

Latin

desolates.

*Meso-*

I forget.

*Neo-*

ˋˋˋ ˋˋˋ ˋˋˋ ˋˋˋˋˋˋ

an act jeweled in parts. Take the plate.
Break it.

# STONE AGE

*"We're going to bomb them back into the Stone Age."* —C. LeMay

*"I never said we should bomb them back to the Stone Age."* —C. LeMay

We set the four boom microphones onstage, and the diva held up to her mouth a trillium, what spelled a word for *dew* dropping over her screen and projected upon its surface: footage from the old night market or Saigon's naval shipyard or the ballad which never truly happened but a cicada-drenched June reverberating up like a choir wherever you went, comrade, and this was a sound which followed into another age of stone, monsoon. I dreamt of the man who refused to say, *I'm sorry,* and then I walked home after another fight in Ithaca, both of us expecting these lamps to flicker on then off as though to signal onstage: *snow,* or a pale curtain of ash. There it was done. Our diva entered her front door, took off her boots, and wept.

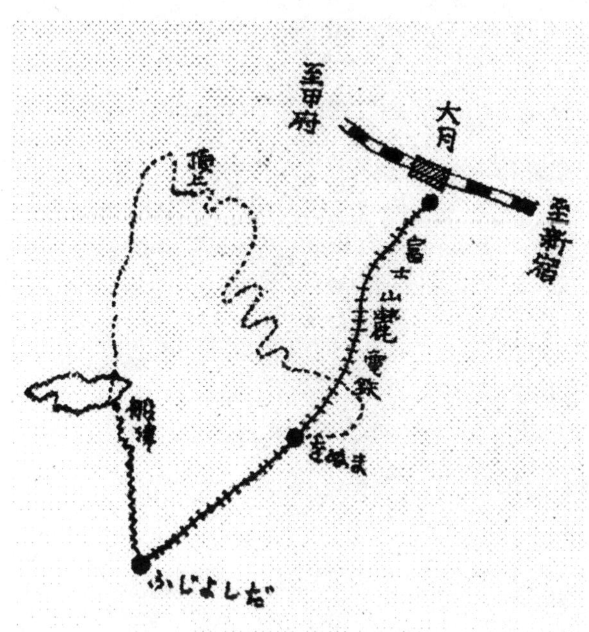
至甲府
大月
至新宿
富士山麓電鉄
ふじよしだ

# DIRGE OF REENACTMENT: PERFORMANCE NOTES

In preproduction, even the wheels are eulogized.

"V" becomes "play."

"Hour" then "Anh," you must say crying.

Meadow, chamomile-dusted, orchid-dusted, one survives.

"Bewilder me."

Twigs and fallen fruit are enacted daily like a malediction.

Fake persimmon tree, opal eyes of buffalo, buffalo-wife made
plural, and washing feet.

The cart has been poached before.

What is peeled, also poached, downpours "và."

Cue striking gourd, a trapdoor of all places.

Who recognizes herself scenically afield? Reed and strings
accompany.

The fallen become tone.

The falcons stalk.

"Đi," if repeated, resounds less and less.

A diva stands behind piercing velvet with long tapestry
needles.

Bells rend salt from skin. Silhouettes descend marking brass.

Such plain notation gestures: Go.

We can wait. Don't worry about ma.

*Flash title card:*

**Đi, đi!**

# SCORE III

# LITANY OF TORTURE

At the museum is a bronze dagger hilt presented as a fragment
looted before any god bound pleasure to books. You swam north.

We had questions. Quickening were years between war then
rumors of people packed into a cave, singing. I know this one.

It starts with the capital not on fire, vengeance: your middle sister
up a date palm. She clamps a blade in her jaw, calling us back.

Across that way, pieces for devotion dim beneath glass, but
what do you mean by this question of music? In our capital,

far without wind or current drawing fists to sand so blue, some
would steal only to feed another. I have no reason for flight.

Our divas tell an entirely different story. Onstage, seven fan out
elbow to elbow. This irony renounces us. So, how about the god

you couldn't recognize, who raised a flag forbidden by color?

There were twenty-four arms and sometimes a thousand. *Take*,
you said with a voice not a song glinting on peace itself. More

crawl today belly-down in grass, waiting for Mother to cross.
She lifts an arm, motions, *go, go*… In the gallery, I recall

gilt bronze buried with our dead. Eternity lies in a box with hammers.
You motion to the guard watching quietly.

# STAR POWER

Though few perform for the canon, one might
dawdle touching a book or two with abandon,
keep herself ceremonious. Hardened, too.

The point is, years ago, I sung a shiny dance
number to that narrow door to destiny.
Behind a door waited many divas wearing

press-on nails. What was wrong with this?
Nothing. They were perfect. In the end,
solos died. Objects died. The diva Quỳnh

released her top fourteen bolero, the closest
to any homecoming, and the number kept
tromping up and downstage. Gaudy feather

boas in a pleasant rhythm. The short answer,
divas sang for you when they sang about joy.

# CHECKLIST

The role goes to galaxy, the divas allude to dying, the triple VHS box sets
go on sale, Ojiisan cuts a cigar, the giraffes going out of focus, I audition
for granddaughter in Ueno Park, the denser exoplanets careen way past
extinction, the Sony station looks on, the loose hair is oiled, the dead lyric,
weighed, the satellites drift beyond beeping and beeping, tables backstage
wobble, the sponsors defend one another, the cue, unclear, the low moon
tumbles, the resin stinks, the paper boat stinks,
grand gestures about keeping a national family
together stake into groaning plots of earth, the
call is coming from below, the trapdoor opens,
returning broken is inevitable, the risk climbs to
dangerous heights, the design eats itself,
smoke goes everywhere beauty destroys.

+

# MONARCH DE JURE

We cannot speak about it, wave a silk sash, pen oblique forecasts bent for trouble.
Who supplicates a thousand-year rule? Clipped to microphones: *đi, đi*          is muffled.

ˆ ˆ ˆ

Chị tám stilettos          'i' in praise, I might exhaust.

Fury has a thin pudding, warm and cold.

ˋˋˋ

You, in lilac, what's your name? Can you go to your mother's house? Does her country welcome you back?

~~~

It's said of our diva, who favored tomatoes toward the end of her life, she brought a silk parasol to her own funeral.

I set fifteen joss sticks in front of her portrait.

Chị tám          so chided, enough. Even praise has a limit.
~~~

# FIGURED BEYOND MEASURE

In this shot, silkworms on mulberry leaf indicate a HYBRID ZONE.

Our theater remains<br>
    standing fractures in the dark          who warbles without smudging her makeup.

A backup dancer pumps away          irrelevant why we cry.

Downstage, a diva, we're shocked by her gown.

Patriotic to which part of exile?—

hoa cúc in the HYBRID ZONE<br>
evokes easy movement. Round

radiant face, I stiffen each part of us leaving.

# INTERSTICES

1.

Huế is not autumn in Paris.

Who cowers, entering the western gates, dressed for a king?

No cabinet's armory fails our Forbidden City.

At thirteen, the boy-king paces unaware in his peony garden.

I have no voice in that, but regarding autumn, scrap my wedding tape.

Đai holds out a fort so long for memories cast.

Simply, I sense our fate in twelve dissimilar ways.

2.

The peony
blossoms auspiciously

on my wedding night.
Though, who's counting?

Grand is she
outside, shirtless,

drying herbs on a line.
Who stays

near the fort
in our red carriage, red

shirt and crown?
Which

cabinet fires
many golden arrows? Glory

to this heart folding.

# SEVENTH FRAME

In this angle, light crawls across the blue
duvet on your bed; I give it

all morning, too, decide what you want from me.

Jupiter greets Orion and then Betelgeuse,
that runaway star in this angle of my dream.

Let's not talk about the boy.

Too many times, I've bartered peace for bells,
wrung a shirt sleeve out to dry on expectation.

In this angle, let's wait in diacritic energy.

Reprisal as a form most difficult to keep. The dais
degrades, tips to both sides. An emperor leaps.

Đai does awaken now bewildered.

Who brought the war to his place, in this angle,
which belfry chimes after all? I'll stay here

as long as I can. Never finish the book.

# IMPERATIVE FOR SHE WHO DELIVERS

1.1 Percussion when Đai leaves unspoken for, wind machine or real as wind.

1.2 Castaway, we have children. Our children go on humming without much.

1.3 Mine haunts out front by the door still painted red, sundried, whose song runs out.

1.4 Hauntingly, Đai returns, a castaway bard. We have children. Glory.

1.5 None return gentle, but mine out front hums. An equinox sun looks down.

2.1 Glorious, apathetic to their suffering, the sun casts our children
with the wind or wind machine—both as real, as devastating as drums.

2.2 I spite the national song one day. I throw reams of sheet music upon
a ravenous hearth. Be this my hearth to spite with, burrows below dirt.

Then, harvest. Books. Flame.

3.1 Simon asphodels—

3.2 Dancers of the court—

3.3 Gone hard with drumming—

3.4 Đai who leaves again—

3.5 Plumes on videotape—

3.6 My shirt sleeve catches—

3.7 Fire plumes alongside—

3.8 Violets offstage—

3.9 A fox in the green, green—

Chthonic. Meadow.

4.1 I remain with this embittered rhythm.

4.2 I remain planting peonies by dusk.

4.3 When Đai returns, I remain borderless.

4.4 Our daughters remain stolen, tortured.

4.5 I remain regarding a face so cursed.

4.6 A fox sits quietly when generous.

4.7 What cannot die has governance, glory.

4.8 We have children. What is mine cannot be beautiful.

4.9 What is mine can never be that beautiful.

5.1 What freezes atop a citadel remains screaming. I remain the child
humming to myself in a cardboard box set in the middle of a room
hours dip in, dip out.

5.2 A countless subject crawls before walking. Subject to whom has
yet broken, hums. I remain crawling through history. Glory, at last,
broken, hums.

6.1 Before his wedding day, Đai reportedly ventures unaccompanied out.

6.2 Past the meadow, through the forest, in a dark den, three tigers vanish.

6.3 Who draws the bowstring taut? Whose imperial subject hurtles near?

6.4 An oracle names that era after gold. Its namesake whips around.

6.5 Who draws our oracle near? Who dares break into the box?

6.6 Perhaps our children can make shoes. Forget the name Đai.

6.7 Late autumn in Huế, by the bridge, I'd like to stop, wash my legs.

6.8 And arms. Sleep where I can, dream about the greatest ocean ever.

# UNDERSCORE

With sudden departure, footprints give minimal sign—evacuate,
all, come down. By journey's end

[đi] [đi]

Fool, you've been put aground, backlit in obscene yellow

[đi] [đi]

Stars compose Divas of Eternal Luminosity. You'll find hope among
ineffable microphones, static lifted to my lips. We,

[đi] [đi]

Hauntology's vast unmaking—hush, don't let them see us

[đi] [đi]

At night filled with easy life, may the book go bedside. Long for
not in Postojna, in a toy train, hollering with joy, my head clean off

[đi] [đi]

Not from mass emigration. Cavernous like heartache, wait

[đi] [đi]

Eros, this show goes on for you and you and you—covet not home
performed through drawn-out ballads; what rhymes

[đi] [đi]

Poignantly offers forgetting. Some forget well. Go on then,

[đi] [đi]

Feel about. How fresh are these prints due river's edge? Describe
with so few words: fearful movement; we might think, malady

[đi] [đi]

An overcoat, cross-collared or blue. Go on then, go

[đi] [đi]

Forget me, cries the silkworm to the mulberry in a fable about grace.
Interpretation: a voluminous choir

[đi] [đi]

In that province of survivor's guilt, come down from here

# CLOVE AND ORANGE

Mid-tempo in nocturne
I studied at the foot          ignoring your calls, one
doubly so—it rained.          Bed sheets with animal
print fell from a line,          bed sheets as curtains
behind us, twisting
description here—muffled          coy—velvet controverts
seasons stripped of color.          You brought dumplings.
You left your car running          outside while I screeched.
End of story. Down the block,

thrown into a box—          shoes, wool jackets had

voices telling someone:          *Go, I hate you.* Fish          sparkled toward the bottom
rung in my dreams. I dreamt          terribly about a novel.          *Get out,* I wanted to say.

*Get out,* said this song          about courage answering
gods of wind. Bare-faced.
Hair, untied through autumn.

# NESOBERANAKATTA

Those are symptoms returning to my chest, of sumac
languor, an occasion folding its pillow longwise. Eyes

obey. One closes to the left like a door. *Come sprawl,*
reads a sign in characters composed entirely of insects.

Emergency contact: a poet, friends in apartments five
state lines west. Soon I'd conjugate shortness of breath.

*Anon,* written in large, irreverent cursive. Who then
waits for a call? Eros? Tsuki? I'd water my plants with

milk, menstrual blood mixed in molasses and pecan. I'd
leave out a stirring spoon. Winter opens on most sides of

crimson. Winter, with such weight, I'd try lying down
by a radiator, by chairs and a table made from good pine.

## INDELIBLE DEVICE

An angled push? Late noon?
Stalked across the yard?
Who bashed eggs at the Honda?

Spectacular, was it hatred
you feared from children
born to citizenry? A bad sign?

A brown paper carton filled with
fruit? Raw trout wrapped in paper?
*If I go,* it said, *visit Ojiisan.*

*Throw his ashes mixed with my ashes*
*up a mountain*—characters in
four straight lines: Tamago?

Ringo? Ketsugo? Arukou?
*—watch out, don't fall.*

# CLOUD ROULETTE

Takes a form on wheels you follow midtown.

Slippers alight sixty frames per second.

As planned, block by block, I cut the slim field.

There, one of us is cruel. Rephrase it—we
        step off any bus
        off any corner
        facing west. Do tell
        how the film's faithful
        to you. In batches—

Color corrected. Can we speak at last?

Blunting each other? Không. My inner seam
        pales in direct sun.

Tell quickly of omens before monsoon.

I sleep on that bus from north to south Không.
Up north to immeasurable torrents.

ˋˋˋ

February, our friend dies. You outline
        a storyboard full
        of his debts, skin, curls.

Tarnish blends on a wet plate you hold then.

Missing a mark assigns secondary
        skips. In Ithaca
        thrown downhill cracks fruit.

But Lucas who throws his body after.

At eighty, my knees hurt like yours once broke
        off a bucking horse.

Sweetest in tall grass with watermelon.

Không, tell no future lovers after me
    I laughed at this scene
    I left when I could.
    I was cruel. Don't search
    the field for what beat
    turning our horses
    loose. Don't save their shoes,
    resoled and painted
    lichen brown. The sun
    sweeps its seventh house.

When you call, our friend is at the station.

Looking like rain, waving his arms around.

## PUMPING

*for Fatima*

I held the summer in two palms

Chapped, a Douglas-fir night

Like its bat throwing bookish

Winds into the door. You burned

What wasn't useful: eggshells

Painted blue so dark they split

Evenly one way or the other

Within eventide's heart, your ritual

Craving a necessary quiet, I

Shrank into that early sitting

Much too close, the bat wheezed

Across your porch, I couldn't help

Yellow jackets swarmed, you said

Fear ran deeper, and a mouse

Finding the bat, gestured

*Go, that way*. I don't remember

How we lived past this season, what

Hardly mattered and you learned to run

Untraceable, wordless without metaphor

Basil in your hair.

# STELLER'S JAY

Half of sharing one acre from your oak to the great
sanded ridge of Eugene herds a dream from stormwater,

that is, how far into the night young swallows would travel
to shelter. In this parable, danger has no shape but larger

birds circle it. Sunday. Your murder is carried over from rumors,
the messenger whose face cannot be true or human though he

speaks in rhythm with his lips. His eyes are tin-blue. Earth
he regards through and through, adopting its posture

incommunicable in any language, the boy whose skin as
a cloth from near galaxies made real. I try to wake,

carry you downstairs, but that boy—not a prophet—is
hatching already colonies of insects through cocoons

before their expression. Fifty pairs of wings. The vision ends.
Your gardens surface a papery sound of moths. Morning.

A second oak has fallen by your home and a bristled,
chucking cry. The spike with blood by your gate

calling an old, bountiful terror—moon-dusted, born
at once, drying their bodies, together.

# SCORE IV

# PARALLELOGRAM

How stunning parts

turn incoherently

tapioca, whirl and bereft, this
makes banishment look easy

baubles, plastic

Suppose diagrams
discontent
disputed maritime territory

figures replete with sirens a ceded
self

sour, febrile launch-ready

Swelling     the wide, intractable
stage for myrrh
                    salted shapes singe

# THIS GRAPHIC IS AN APRICOT

Passing for local, therefore, accented
on VHS. I draw umbrellas.

Some pass a troupe, accent-grave.
By Kindergarten

air invokes nostalgia bedazzling divos.
Still, the joy is out to tango,

sticky, set to Parisienne-
Vietnamese, I sing as my mother sings.

Look, I'm singing. Trompe l'œil,
the homage, a lamppost off-

key: Hà nội ơi
in downpour, reverb, one divo

at the microphone set to lingua
franca passing for peace. An accent

is not an accent
plucked from eucalyptus. Go

to your worst hour the interlude
suggests. I'll be here

looking through rain for the children.

# OPEN FIRE

*a tempo rubato*

The coda's already given up in our singing.
December, Ithaca. Purple finches
batter into a car singing. Phenomenal pain

blazons person to person who's running
dressed in a wooded costume. You rent
the studio apartment above mine.

Who batters through it turning an instrument
palm out and humming, "Stop, come here,"
who writes and takes off entering fog knowingly?

Few might enter with a pinch of salt. Few
so troubled might read "Speech" as "Salt,"
lip-sync "Salt," drop by an oak

watching eternity turpentine and scorch
the coffee. It did on a day I brought
those finches in. Your grandmother called.

Panicle of pellet holes embedded yet
familiar, few would pause before going home,
devotedly and markedly kiss every door.

# COURIER

There's a word for migration stuck in assent. The word
glints like an addressee, jealous. I pronounce, "Ambulatory"

in a tone hexagonal, de-winged, though the sky says, "Well,
what do we say about that?" And Dahlia's bathing outside.

Drones overhead. Summer pine in lowercase. Fairy lights
adorn the tin bath. Tarragon. Jasmine. Alone, I fear

tumbling out front of that image. Chickadees swoop seeds
so ruby, I tell it slant, "Welcome. Where I'm from, a squall

pitches forward." Dahlia dries her hair on the frost-bitten
porch, which means another word for "Post Office."

We haven't danced in decades together. Reznikoff waits
on a branch through the storm. Here's a note on dying.

Deliverance in lowercase. Right. Where I'm from, bombs
aren't signed with a pink Sharpie. No one dances at night.

# MEMENTO: 108 BPM

Plus one, bà ngoại counts an early life wend- ing counterclockwise

thread, into which I count empty lotus pods for the summer

in Saigon, where she vaults an appointment with death. I can't join

a sharp chromatic dawn like hers, the end, bent cricket legs, who

sits beside telling the wrong story to everyone; ông ngoại

lights a cigarette in his portrait. Some, not all of us, wear

rainfall, clip-on gold earrings and bangles to his funeral.

Luck plays alive well,        unhurried, and mer-        ciful. Luck takes out
her teeth at a shrine        where ông ngoại's portrait        sits next to the wrong
story once more. We,        not half of us, leave        oranges, plates of
candy for our dead        I count aloud. Luck        boards last wearing red.
Forgive her, there she        goes to an old, old        earth, swept with the beads
rustling with all good        intention. Forgive        where she forgets
so far from beauty        I adore even        those hands on your lap.

# WEB BETWEEN

*D.C. al Segno*

Oof, this is my broken foot.
I broke it at home, ma, last night
in our glossary of memory.
Don't worry. I'm soft. I stay
soft in this country.
Would you believe "intention of
genocide," Sartre's tribunal,
key to key, tree to force
ligamentous not large, Tennyson's
"earth" or "Ay!" as you say,
"Ay!" in this
fluorescent room
heaving Radnóti's earth?
Verbs recover me
miraculous with a diva
whose name meant, once,
celebration. Shirt on a line
put together
no one begged like you.

# CATEGORIES: LIGHT AND CHALK

In this glossary of something else,
    I put my energy into the unconditional
repertoire of fondness
    as we wept at the close of Ghibli's *Kaguya-*

*hime* in the theater where we also debated
    if language could truly
appear in exile,
    and my friend took
that second job after graduating.

    Every morning
I saw her hands folded
    under the sheet, and the pain
near her belly, what was once
    an archaeologist labeled, prehistoric,

or what leapt off the pier
    with a skeleton
in my country,

    or, into that scene of it,
a seer with her bones jangling about.

    Such vibrations didn't matter,
but a wandering
    through the subterranean streams,
of anklets

    at the border nearing
my mother's nation and this one.

    I recognized love
for what you were
    in this icy desert like the deft
hands which spelled out, "vả,"
    in Vietnamese, or the word "and"
that accidental exit
    moving away in this accidental sound,

as you said,
    that boat was no longer her story;
or to wait,

an hourglass of torture.

How did *vả*
extend beyond our waiting?

Who was there, afloat upon
this ambulating
line or tarragon of pulp
to spell out these whole

butcheries of speech;

how could I carve
these moments in your likeness,
asked an oracle of bone,
but then the people looked up
from their parted seas, and out of that,
a fishing boat,
what loosened us beyond the ridge?

It doesn't matter, you said,
the archaeologist falling asleep.
I stared into Mars

beyond somewhere outside,
the head-on red
collision, what couldn't wake
us either.

# SCORE V

# CAST OFF BÀ NGOẠI

This portrait glows velvet soft.

Her granite palisade is a word for
beseech. *Ask harder,* it means.

Much is dull about the day among
days past her funeral.

You dream about her country, no.

A speech delivered on television.
There it is, in Technicolor.

An eon of ordinary torture
propped like stones at her altar.

I sing about no one, you say.

In this dream, I sing as if online,
as if at a distant, booming.

## ["THIS DOOR WE BOTH ENTERED"]

HOST in velvet
plum tuxedo +
HOST in glassy
heels, Swarovski
brooch + Saigon
hair coiffed
oceanic. *Alright,*
*you were there* +
HOST teases
HOST in formal
"you" + third person
+ a tortoise moving
between earth and
sky, a thousand
holy doors + pick
one, you tell me
+ waving up
like this door
might wave back.

# OVERGROWTH AS TORUS

In the bicycle factory, in what used to make one
    state-issued vehicle per household

In which you, standing by its back mortared wall

In Metelkova with a harp, pink strobes tapping orbs

In which I knelt and fainted mid-performance

In the performance, from somewhere beyond my body
    I began to scream, in the screaming

Offstage, a lover who set herself on fire, no,
    I couldn't touch paper for weeks

Dovan, who came with music, barley stew

We sat around not saying much, agreed

In paradise you gifted, on different occasions, a rose,

the first mistakenly synthetic; it wasn't a reading

Dovan rode bicycles named Dovan or Drone

In which we kissed night on the bridge taking turns, I lit
wild moss, in which the performance might've destroyed

Where could it end driving around witching hours

Do you think of us now and the wet lantern path
beside the river, I do

# THE ARBORIST

Strong as a day of swallows
swept from reeds on

24th and Spirit of St. Stephens,
one fraction meant peppermint.

Ezra pulled blocks of thistle.
*Take care,* said an ex

at the end, so cruel. Even
Dobermans went flat

looking like violets.
A prophecy went cold.

Troughs of desert rain. Quail toes
pattered years off the map.

I washed underwear outside
during that era. I kissed thirteen

people. Extremity's undoing.
What more can be said about

death, otherwise, before
the green thread of protest?

Then, I might've set myself
afire though

all my friends were there,
and all my friends have gone.

No, keep humming. In another
country, everyone is free.

# FIGURE EIGHT

River of neglect, bring us far.

Ma curls up at eight without books.

She, without receipts, layers time.

Time, she says and stops at this word.

You know she means far north of us.

Holding grief suspended on fractals.

Neither feral nor swept aside.

Look, she says, we lie down. America.

Don't be scared. April's black cloud.

May the occupants surrender.

Persist with their dying, music recounts.

Every invasion occupies. Ma says,

*I'm scared for you, going out like that.*

*Are you sick? Call when you're home.*

Far north, I'm told, women look like me.

An oracle laying out these signs.

Cascara bark and four of coins. Et cetera.

I'll pass them over when it's time.

# LYCHEE PEELER

*a projective aubade*

Emblematic, this holy door behind us

though not once do you climb from Enola's
center nose seat, who cries over light

stuck on syllables—*em*

*và em*—must speak unspoken for, so
you're feverish, flinging up allegories.

Herons go upstage the color of lychee.

In one allegory, behind the door's another
dog; the dog says little but wears a look:

the door's no more holy than you.

Who flees south? What did the dog say?
Half a dozen mines in our theater of brass.

A Superfortress Boeing, an oracle, no?

Then, you curse aground, walk offstage.
Divas grimace beautifully with their hands.

An oxcart is draped in rope, banana leaves.

I murmur—*em*—I can confirm the dog
last in your dream carried on like

one who checks on clouds every morning.

# ENCORE

But the synopsis to music in exile
claimed too much:
look, how our mothers suffer.

Duras or Đan Nguyên, praise
to the DIVO, props pumped away
tuning an outline of our temple

dark. Pizzicato vibrated onstage.
Flutes welded to seas
some were shocked by. Too,

music charged itself on tape.
Declension's rehearsal. Rosy at last.
Bún, ò, radiantly hoofed,

would cast several parts of us leaving.
In the hall, I stiffened in the dark.
Who are you? What do you want?

## CRAFT TALK

An open letter to fear,
seek not an answer

but the red curtain
rising on cue,

a seascape painted
gold. Danger

comes and goes.
Let the screaming

scream all they want.
Don't stick around

for any peace talk.
Wheels of fortune

make sturdy lines,
as do birches,

honeysuckle, and kin.
Arrange what known

history stays
marginal, askance,

held unceremoniously
beloved. Pardon

the blood. We know not
medicine marked

for genocide.
Every night, fast

with a world rationed.
Don't look away.

Annihilation is that
song bent for dignity.

Here's a chorus
between trees

from olive to banyan,
what was ours

became yours. No need
to silence any burning flag:

*What do we want—*
*When do we want it—*

Yes, an open letter can be
just if we try. Set sail

with nothing but skin,
sugar to our names.

connaître

5) Connaissez-vous ces homme? — Non, je n'en connais aucun.

6) Nul en ce monde n'est sans défaut.

の文字が黒板に見ゆ

失敗々々ニ重寘シ

文学士櫻井教授をパケリ

フランス語の教師

ジュネ パー

# CLOSED CAPTIONING

*an intarsia*

Divas manifold
sharing little, endure because of language

[à]

Done, carried out [boat-dust], [wind machine]

[à]

Raising applause from our dead

[à]

Grown cypress behind
rainfall degrees hotter on that planet

[à]

You destroy [long ago]

[à]

The great national audience

[à]

Pastoral, edict, preposition
terre à terre

[à]

Section B, Row 45

[à]

Larks having been shaped topographically [banned]

[à]

Odd hours of a night
you laugh, clapping, but don't know why

[à]

Milk on betel leaf

[à]

Costume outline [muddy, offstage]

[à]

[Diaphanous] raising bells, "distant-you"
chime across

[à]

Eucalyptus to behold us

[à]

Cursing ["xa xa xa lắm"]

# ORACULAR MALADIES

## ACKNOWLEDGMENTS

Big thanks to editors of the following journals for first publishing these poems.

*Annulet*: "Web Between," "Closed Captioning"
*Cobra Milk*: "Clove and Orange," "Nesoberanakatta," "Indelible Device"
*Dialogist*: "Dirge of Reenactment: Performance Notes"
*Four Way Review*: "Residual"
*Firmament* (Sublunary Editions): "Spear Bearer"
*Gulf Coast*: "Score V // Cast Off Bà Ngoại," ["This Door We Both Entered"]
*Harvard Review*: ["Mai, the dawn!"]
*In Parentheses*: "This Graphic Is an Apricot"
*jubilat*: "Stone Age"
*La Piccioletta Barca*: "Interstices"
*mercury firs*: "Cloud Roulette," "Pumping," "Steller's Jay"
*Nat. Brut*: "Categories: Light and Chalk"
*New Orleans Review*: "Score III // Litany of Torture"
*Pamenar Magazine*: "Monarch de Jure," "Figured beyond Measure," "The Cellist," "Oracles, Untended"
*Pinwheel*: ["Who ghost-locks me?"], ["How might you be attentive to my living?"], ["Mesh is pink, taffeta bedazzled"], ["Can you describe the sound?"], ["Through burnt canopies, a footnote whistles overhead"]
*Quarterly West*: "Score I // En Eminence"
*Shō Poetry Journal*: "Suppose a Lute," ["Xa Xa Xa Lắm"]

PHOTO: KRISTINA ROSE

SOPHIA TERAZAWA is the author of the novel, *Tetra Nova* (Deep Vellum, US; the87press, UK/Ireland) and two poetry collections, *Winter Phoenix* (Deep Vellum) and *Anon* (Deep Vellum), along with chapbooks, *I AM NOT A WAR* (Essay Press) and *Correspondent Medley* (Factory Hollow Press), winner of the 2018 Tomaž Šalamun Prize.